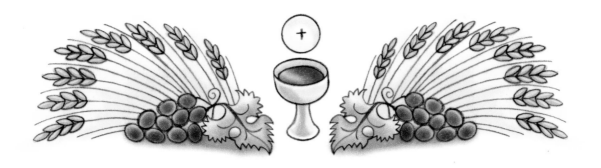

Presented to

_____

for your First Holy Communion

On _____

With love and prayers always,

_____

*"I have called you by name,
you are mine."*

(Isaiah 43:1)

My First Communion

REMEMBRANCE BOOK

Written by Joan Marie Arbogast

Illustrated by Veronica Walsh

Pauline
BOOKS & MEDIA
Boston

ISBN 0-8198-4916-2

Book design by Mary Joseph Peterson, FSP

Illustrated by Veronica Walsh

Published by Pauline Books & Media, 50 Saint Pauls Avenue, Boston, MA 02130-3491

Printed in Korea.

MFCR SIPSKOGUNKYO9-8054 4916-2

www.pauline.org

Pauline Books & Media is the publishing house of the Daughters of St. Paul, an international congregation of women religious serving the Church with the communications media.

2 3 4 5 6 7 8 9   19 18 17 16

Contents

I Prepared for
My First Holy Communion

Family Who Helped Me
Prepare for This Day

Draw or attach photos of family members who helped you prepare for your First Holy Communion. (You might include parents, siblings, grandparents, aunts, uncles, or cousins.) Write about how they helped you.

"*Prepare the way of the Lord, make his paths straight.*"

(Mark 1:3)

3

Others Who Helped Me Prepare

Draw or attach photos of those who helped you prepare for
your First Holy Communion: friends, teachers, priests, sisters . . .
Write about how they helped you.

I Prepared by Receiving
the Sacrament of Reconciliation

Before receiving the precious Body and Blood of Christ,
I asked forgiveness for my sins.

Forgive me, Jesus, for I have sinned.
I am sorry I hurt you and others with my words
 and actions.
Please help me to love you with my whole heart, soul,
 and being.
And help me to love others as you do.
Thank you for loving me always.
Thank you for forgiving my sins.
This I pray. Amen.

I received

the

Sacrament of Reconciliation

for the first time

on _____

at _____ Parish

in _____.

As the Good Shepherd, Jesus calls us back to him when we are lost. Every time we receive the Sacrament of Reconciliation we grow closer to Jesus.

Now that you made your First Reconciliation, draw your "lamb" in the "flock" that follows the Good Shepherd.

"My sheep hear my voice.
I know them, and they follow me."

(John 10:27)

I Prepared by Learning about Symbols of the Eucharist

The Eucharist is the Real Presence of Jesus. The Church uses many images or symbols to remind us of the Eucharist.

Draw the symbols used for the Eucharist in the banners below. Then circle the symbols used on your First Holy Communion banner.

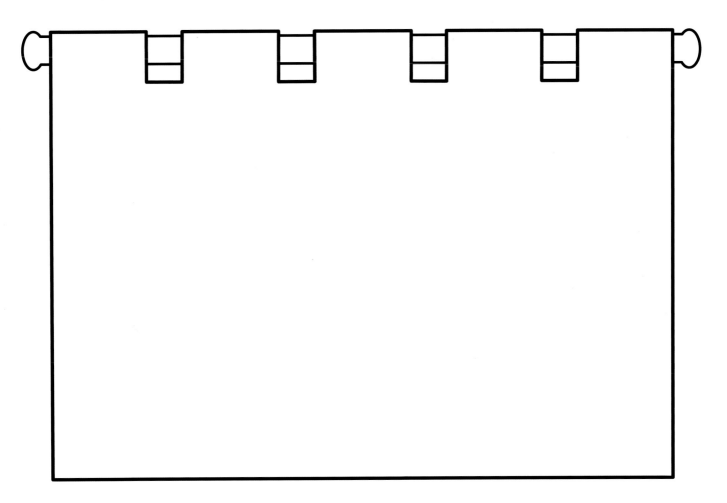

Wheat and Grapes

Wheat is a grain used to make bread. Grapes are a fruit used to make wine. Together, the wheat and grapes are a symbol for the bread and wine that become the sacred Body and Blood of Christ during Mass.

Host and Chalice

We see this symbol often. We see it on banners. We see it in stained glass windows. We find it on First Communion cards, too. It reminds us of the Body and Blood of Christ we receive in the Eucharist. Sometimes the host is marked with a cross. It reminds us that Jesus died for our sins.

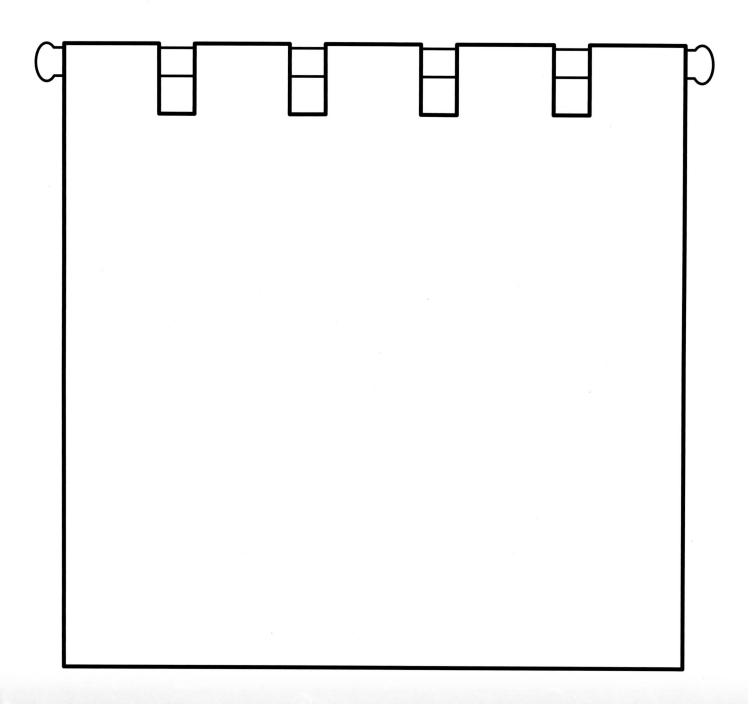

Loaves and Fishes

This symbol reminds us of a Bible story. It reminds us of a miracle Jesus performed when he turned five loaves and two fishes into enough food to feed a large crowd. At Mass, Jesus feeds us with his Body and Blood. The loaves and fishes are one of the oldest symbols for the Eucharist.

Broken Loaf of Bread and Cup of Wine

At the Last Supper, Jesus celebrated the Eucharist for the first time with his apostles. He took a loaf of bread. He blessed it. He broke it. He gave it to his apostles. He told them, "This is my Body, which will be given up for you." Then he blessed the wine and gave it to his apostles. He said, "This is my Blood. Do this in memory of me." Catholic Christians do this at every Mass.

Altar, Bread, and Wine

These symbols remind us of the bread and wine that are offered on the altar at Mass. When the priest consecrates our gifts of bread and wine, they become the Body and Blood of Christ.

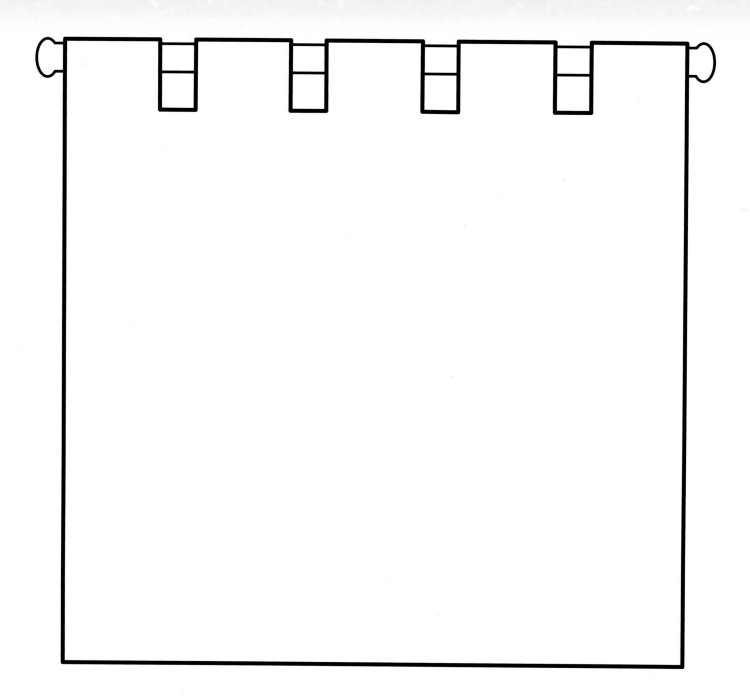

Priest Raising the Host

This symbol reminds us of a special part of the Mass. It is called the consecration. When the priest prays the words of consecration, the host becomes the Body of Christ that we receive. The wine becomes the Blood of Christ that we receive.

I Prepared with a Special Retreat

A *retreat* is a special "time apart" for thinking about God and praying to him, for listening to God and growing closer to him.

List some of the things you did during your retreat. (You might include singing, praying, listening to stories, making crafts, or sharing a special meal.)

_____

_____

_____

_____

Keepsakes from the Retreat

Attach keepsakes here.

"Jesus took with him Peter and John and James,
and went up on the mountain to pray."

(Luke 9:28)

Draw a picture of your favorite activity during the retreat or attach more keepsakes.

My First Holy Communion Mass

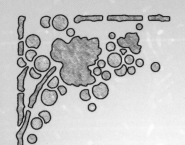
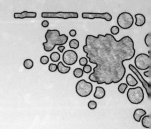

The Invitation

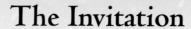

My family invited relatives and friends to share in the joy of my First Holy Communion Mass.

Attach the invitation or announcement below.

"Praise the LORD!
O give thanks to the LORD, for he is good;
for his steadfast love endures forever."

(Psalm 106:1)

Today, _____,

I, _____,

received the

Body and Blood of Jesus

for the first time

at _____ Mass

at _____ Parish

in _____.

Mass was celebrated by

Father _____.

21

Entrance Song: _____

First Reading: _____

Responsorial Psalm: _____

Second Reading: _____

Gospel: _____

Offertory Song: _____

Communion Song: _____

Recessional Song: _____

Circle your favorite song.

Did you have a special role in the Mass such as presenting an offertory gift, reading from Scripture, or reading the petitions? If so, record it here.

_____

_____

_____

"For as often as you eat this bread and drink the cup, you proclaim the Lord's death until he comes."

(1 Corinthians 11:26)

The Liturgy of the Word

The priest welcomed all who came to celebrate the Eucharist. He welcomed family, relatives, and friends. Then we listened to the Word of God.

Draw a picture of the Gospel story you heard.

"The word is near you, on your lips and in your heart."

(Romans 10:8)

The Presentation and Preparation of the Gifts

God blesses each of us with many gifts.

During this part of the Mass, we offer our gifts back to God. We offer the gifts of bread and wine. They become the Body and Blood of Jesus.

Throughout the ages, bread has been a basic food for people around the world. It has been shared during mealtimes, around tables, and with people we love. At our Eucharistic meal, we share the Bread of Life.

Wine has also been shared at mealtimes throughout the ages. It has been served at joyful events like weddings, banquets, and our Eucharistic meals.

We offer other gifts, too. Most importantly, we offer the gift of ourselves.

Today I offered these gifts to Jesus.

Draw the gifts offered in the boxes below.

*"I will offer to you a thanksgiving sacrifice
and call on the name of the LORD."*

(Psalm 116:17)

The Consecration

The consecration is like taking part in the Last Supper. Jesus invited his apostles to take and eat the bread, which had become his Body. He also invited his apostles to take and drink the cup of wine, which had become his Blood. Jesus told them, "Do this in memory of me." This is what we do at Mass.

When the priest holds up the Host and the chalice, we silently pray, "My Lord and my God!" because the bread and wine are now the Body and Blood of Christ.

Color in the stained glass window design below.

"I am the living bread that came down from heaven."

(John 6:51)

The Lord's Prayer

Jesus taught his disciples how to pray the Our Father.
He taught them the same words we pray.

Our Father, who art in heaven,
hallowed be thy name;
thy kingdom come,
thy will be done
on earth as it is in heaven.
Give us this day our daily bread,
and forgive us our trespasses,
as we forgive those who trespass against us;
and lead us not into temptation,
but deliver us from evil.
Amen.

What is your favorite part of the Our Father? On the lines below, write your favorite line. Then write why you like it.

_____

_____

_____

_____

Sharing Christ's Peace

At the Last Supper, Jesus told his disciples, *"Peace I leave with you; my peace I give you. I do not give to you as the world gives. Do not let your hearts be troubled, and do not let them be afraid"* (John 14:27).

At Mass, the priest offers us the peace of Christ. We in turn offer a sign of that peace to those around us.

In the space below, trace your hand. List ways you offer the peace of Christ to your family and friends at home and school.

"So when you are offering your gift at the altar, if you remember that your brother or sister has something against you, leave your gift there before the altar and go; first be reconciled to your brother or sister, and then come and offer your gift."

(Matthew 5:23–24)

Lamb of God

After we offer others the sign of peace, we pray or sing the Lamb of God. In the Bible, John the Baptist calls Jesus the Lamb of God. This means that Jesus is the sacrifice offered to God to take away our sins.

At Mass, as the priest breaks the bread, we pray three times that Jesus is the Lamb of God, the one whose death takes away our sins. The first two times we ask him to have mercy on us. The third time we ask him to give us his peace.

Color the picture below.

Prayer Before Receiving Jesus

Before Communion the priest raises the Host. Aloud, we tell Jesus that we are not worthy to have him come to us. We also tell him that we trust that his word is enough to heal us.

We also pray silently.

We ask for God's forgiveness.

We ask for God's blessing.

We pray for others, too.

Record your prayer below.

Dear Jesus,

_____

_____

_____

_____

This I pray. In the name of the Father, and of the Son, and of the Holy Spirit. Amen.

Prayer After Receiving Jesus

After we receive Communion, we silently thank Jesus for coming to us.

We thank him for the many blessings we have received.

We ask him to help us live as his disciples.

We ask him to bless others in need of his help.

Record your prayer below.

Dear Jesus,

_____

_____

_____

_____

This I pray. In the name of the Father, Son, and Holy Spirit. Amen.

"O give thanks to the LORD,
for he is good;
for his steadfast love
endures for ever."

(1 Chronicles 16:34)

The Final Blessing

At the end of Mass, the priest blesses all those who gathered for Mass. He tells us to go in peace and to give glory to God by the way we live.

We respond, "Thanks be to God!"

In the footprints below, write or draw how you plan to give glory to God.

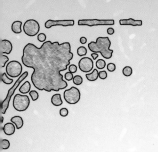
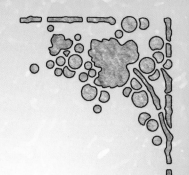

My Favorite Memory of
My First Holy Communion

On the blank lines below, record your favorite memory of this extra-special Mass. Think about how you felt after receiving Holy Communion, or how you felt having your family and friends share this sacrament with you.

_____

_____

_____

_____

Attach your favorite photo here.

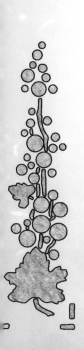
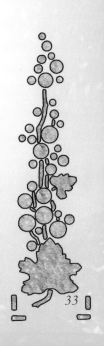

Celebration of
My First Holy Communion

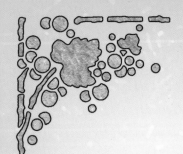
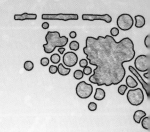

Special Day, Special Clothing

Today is an extra special day. It is the day I receive the Body and Blood of Jesus for the very first time.

When I was baptized, I wore white clothes as a symbol of my new life in Christ.

Today too, I wear something special as I come to the Lord's Table for the first time.

Attach a photo here.

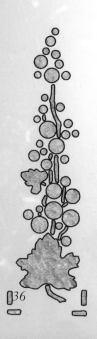

" . . . for in Christ Jesus you are all children of God through faith. As many of you as were baptized into Christ have clothed yourselves with Christ."

(Galatians 3:26–27)

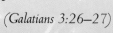

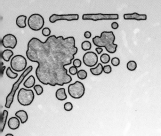
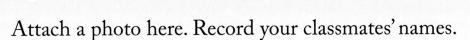

My First Communion Class Photo

Attach a photo here. Record your classmates' names.

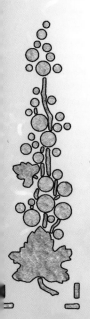
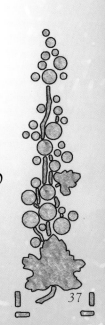

"The LORD bless you and keep you; the LORD make his face to shine upon you, and be gracious to you; the LORD lift up his countenance upon you, and give you peace."

(Numbers 6:24–26)

Autographs of Friends Who Made Their First Holy Communion

" . . . let your light shine before others, so that they may see your good works and give glory to your Father in heaven."

(Matthew 5:16)

Afterward, My Family Celebrated

We met at _____.

We shared a special meal of _____

_____.

Favorite foods were _____

_____.

We decorated our table with _____

_____.

Other decorations were _____

_____.

Our family customs for celebrating First Holy Communion

include _____

_____

_____.

Some of My Favorite Photos of the Celebration

Place some photos of your celebration on these pages.

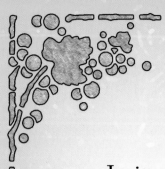
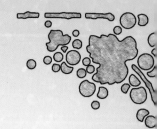

Guests and Greetings

Invite your guests to write a message for you below.

"Therefore encourage one another and build up each other,
as indeed you are doing."

(1 Thessalonians 5:11)

Gifts Received

Gift	From	Thank You Sent
_____	_____	☐
_____	_____	☐
_____	_____	☐
_____	_____	☐
_____	_____	☐
_____	_____	☐
_____	_____	☐
_____	_____	☐
_____	_____	☐

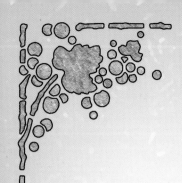
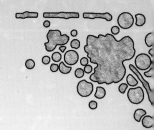

Special Cards or Letters
from My Parents and Siblings

Attach cards and letters below.

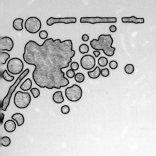
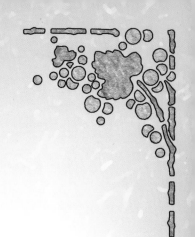

Special Cards or Letters
from My Grandparents

Attach cards and letters below.

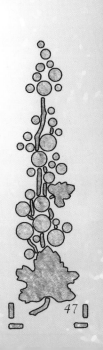

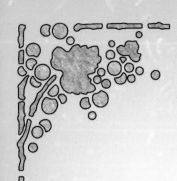
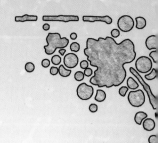

Special Cards or Letters
from My Godparents

Attach cards and letters below.

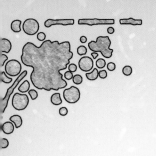
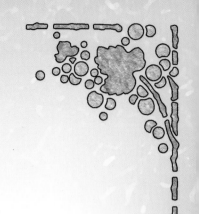

Special Cards or Letters
from My Teachers

Attach cards and letters below.

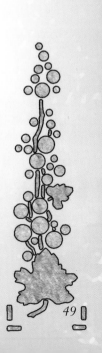

From This Day Forward . . .

Today, in the presence of my family and friends,
I received Jesus in the Eucharist for the first time.
Now that I can participate more fully in the Mass,
I want to receive Jesus in Holy Communion every

_____.

I know the sacraments help me to grow in faith.
They help me to grow closer to Jesus, too. I know I will
make mistakes along the way. But I also know that I
can receive forgiveness for my sins in the Sacrament of
Reconciliation. I plan to receive this sacrament every

_____.

Baptism, Eucharist, and Confirmation are the three
Sacraments of Initiation. When I have received all
three of these sacraments, I will be a full member of the
Church. Now, I want to keep learning and growing in
faith and drawing closer to Jesus. I plan to do this by

_____

_____

_____.

The Story of the Eucharist

Manna in the Desert

God chose Moses to lead his people from slavery in Egypt to the Promised Land. They traveled by night and day. To guide his people, God lit the night sky with a streak of fire. During the day, he led them with a column of clouds.

Day after day, year after year, Moses led his people. But after a while, the people grew more hungry and more tired. They complained, "We don't have enough to eat."

God heard their complaining. He told Moses, "Tell the people that I will send them meat this evening. And I will send them bread in the morning. I will do this so they know I am God." He also instructed Moses, "Tell your people that they should gather only enough food for a day."

That evening, God sent quail. Everyone ate until they were filled.

In the morning, God sent manna. It looked like wafers and tasted sweet like honey.

On the sixth day of the week, Moses told the people to gather enough food for two days. "There will be no manna on the seventh day," said Moses. "It is the Lord's Day, a day of rest." So the people did as Moses had told them. They gathered food enough for two days.

On the Sabbath, there was no manna. The people ate what they had gathered the day before.

For forty years, Moses led his people. Throughout their journey, God sent bread from heaven. He nourished them every step of the way.

— Taken from Exodus 16

Something to think about . . . We, too, are on a journey. Heaven is our Promised Land. God provides us with food for our journey. How can we thank him for his constant love?

_____

_____

_____

Elijah, the Prophet: God Provides

Elijah was a prophet. A prophet is someone who speaks for God, often to call people back to God. Elijah loved God with all his heart.

Elijah lived during the time when Ahab was king of Israel. The king worshiped idols made of metal and stone. He called these idols Baal.

Elijah told King Ahab, "There is only one, true God." But the king wouldn't listen. He ordered his people to worship Baal, too.

This upset Elijah. He told King Ahab, "As long as you worship idols, there will be no rain to water the land."

Soon, the ground dried up. Plants and animals died. People grew hungry and thirsty.

Yet, God provided water from a brook for Elijah. God provided food, too. Every morning and evening, God sent ravens to Elijah. The birds brought him bread and meat.

Without rain, the brook slowed to a trickle. Eventually, the brook went dry. Even the ravens stopped coming. But God took care of Elijah. God told him to visit a widow who would give him bread.

Elijah did what God had told him. He found the woman and asked for some bread. But the woman told him, "I have very little flour and oil. I won't have enough to feed you, myself, and my son."

"Do not worry," Elijah told her. "God will provide enough."

The widow did as the prophet had said. She baked bread for him. She was surprised that she had enough flour and oil to bake bread for Elijah, for herself, and for her son!

Day after day, she made bread.

Day after day, God provided all that they needed.

— Taken from 1 Kings 17

Something to think about . . . How does God provide for you? How do you trust God?

_____

_____

_____

The Birth of Jesus

One day, God sent the angel Gabriel to Mary. He told her she would have a son and name him Jesus. He would be the Son of God.

Mary didn't understand the angel. But she said, "I will do whatever God asks me to do."

When it came time to have the baby, Mary went with Joseph to Bethlehem. It was crowded with people. There were no rooms where the Holy Family could stay. So Mary and Joseph stayed in a stable. That's where Jesus was born.

Mary wrapped her newborn baby in swaddling clothes and laid him in a manger. Mary and Joseph named him Jesus, just as the angel had said.

Later, an angel appeared to shepherds. He told them that the Son of God was born. He told them they could find the baby lying in a manger. Then a choir of angels sang a beautiful song. "Glory to God in the highest, and peace on earth to people of good will."

As soon as the angels left, the shepherds hurried to Bethlehem. They wanted to see the newborn King of kings.

After the shepherds saw baby Jesus, they praised God. They thanked him, too.

Then they hurried to tell others about the good news!

— Taken from Luke 1:26–2:20

Something to think about . . . We know that God loves us. He gave us the greatest gift of all time, the gift of his Son, Jesus. What gifts do you want to give God? Write them in the boxes below.

Jesus Multiplies Loaves and Fishes

One day, a large crowd followed Jesus and his apostles to Bethsaida. They listened as he talked about the kingdom of God.

Some asked Jesus to heal them.

And Jesus did.

As the morning turned to afternoon, the apostles told him, "You should dismiss the people so they can go find food."

"There is no need to send them away," replied Jesus. "Feed them yourselves."

The apostles were confused. There were at least five thousand men, plus women and children. How could they possibly feed them?

"We don't have enough food," they told him. "And we don't have enough money to buy that much food."

Then Andrew, one of the apostles, told Jesus, "A little boy here has five loaves of bread and two fishes."

Jesus told his apostles, "Have everyone sit." Then Jesus took the loaves and fishes. He looked up to heaven and said a blessing. He broke the bread and gave it to his apostles to pass out to the crowd. They also passed out the fishes.

Everyone ate until they were satisfied.

When the apostles gathered the leftovers, there were enough to fill twelve baskets.

The people were amazed at what Jesus had done.

— Taken from Luke 9:10–17 and John 6:5–15

Something to think about . . . If you were in the crowd that day, what would you have said or done?

_____

_____

_____

"I Am the Bread of Life"

Jesus and his apostles traveled to Capernaum. The crowd followed him there. They found him teaching in a synagogue. They asked Jesus, "What sign will you give us so we can believe in you?"

Jesus told them, "I am the bread of life. Whoever comes to me will never be hungry." Then he added, "Whoever believes in me will never be thirsty."

People wondered how Jesus could say such things.

He explained, "I am the bread that came down from heaven. Whoever eats this bread will live forever."

Still, people wondered.

Still, they were confused.

So Jesus told them, "Those who eat my flesh and drink my blood have eternal life, and I will raise them up on the last day."

Then he added, "Those who eat my flesh and drink my blood live in me and I live in them."

— Taken from John 6:22–58

Something to think about . . . We can't understand everything about the mystery of the Eucharist. But we can praise and thank God for the gift of his Son. Write your own prayer of thanks below.

_____

_____

_____

The Last Supper

The night before Jesus died on the cross, he met with his apostles for a Passover meal in Jerusalem. It would be the last meal they would share before he suffered, died, and rose for the sins of the world. It would be a very special meal.

Jesus told his apostles, "I am eager to share this Passover meal with you."

At supper, he took the Passover bread in his hands. He blessed it, broke it, and gave it to his apostles. He told them, "Take and eat; this is my body."

Then Jesus took the Passover wine. He gave thanks to God, the Father. He gave the cup to his apostles and said, "Drink from it, all of you. This is my blood of the covenant, which is poured out for many for the forgiveness of sins." He told them, "Do this in remembrance of me."

After dinner, they sang a final song. Then the apostles went with Jesus to the Mount of Olives.

— Taken from Matthew 26: 26–30 and Luke 22:14–20

❧

Something to think about . . . Today we share the same gift Jesus shared with his apostles. We share the gift of the Eucharist, the Body and Blood of Christ. And we end our celebration with song, just like the apostles did. What are some of your favorite worship songs? List them below.

_____

_____

_____

Bread for the Journey

On Easter Sunday, two of Jesus's disciples were walking from Jerusalem to Emmaus. Jesus appeared beside them. At first, they didn't recognize him. They were busy talking about all that had happened. They told him how Jesus had suffered and died. They told him that angels had appeared to the women who went to visit the tomb. And they told him that the body of Jesus was not there.

Jesus listened as they walked toward Emmaus. He also explained the Scriptures to them as they walked.

Soon day turned to evening. The disciples invited him to stay and have dinner with them. And he did.

At dinner, Jesus took the bread and blessed it. He broke it and gave it to the disciples. That's when the disciples recognized Jesus. But then Jesus disappeared.

Immediately the disciples returned to Jerusalem to tell the other disciples the good news!

— *Taken from Luke 24:13–15*

Something to think about . . . Today you received Jesus in Holy Communion for the first time. What "good news" will you share with your family and friends? Write it on the lines below.

_____

_____

_____

"Feed My Sheep"

After Jesus rose from the dead, he appeared to his disciples again and again.

He appeared to Mary of Magdala at the tomb. He called her by name. "Mary," he said.

Then she recognized him. "Teacher," she cried.

Later, Jesus appeared to his disciples who were hiding behind locked doors. "Peace be with you," said Jesus.

His disciples were amazed.

Another time, Jesus shared breakfast with his disciples. He took bread and fish. He gave it to them to eat. After breakfast, Jesus asked Simon Peter, "Do you love me more than the others?"

"Yes, Lord," Simon replied.

Jesus asked him a second time . . . and a third time.

All three times, Simon Peter replied, "Yes."

Each time, Jesus told him, "Feed my sheep."

Finally, Jesus told him, "Follow me."

And Simon Peter did.

— Taken from John 20-21

Something to think about . . . Jesus wants us to follow him, too. Think of the things you do and say that show that you are a disciple of Jesus. Write them on the lines below.

_____

_____

_____

Other Bible Stories I Know

List some of the other Bible stories you know on the lines below.

_____

_____

_____

_____

_____

_____

"But Jesus called for them and said,
'Let the little children come to me, and do not stop them;
for it is to such as these that the kingdom of God belongs.'"

(Luke 18:16)

My Prayers

❧ Sign of the Cross

In the name of the Father,
and of the Son,
and of the Holy Spirit. Amen.

❧ Hail Mary

Hail Mary, full of grace,
the Lord is with you.
Blessed are you among women,
and blessed is the fruit of your womb, Jesus.
Holy Mary, Mother of God,
pray for us sinners,
now and at the hour of our death. Amen.

✒ Our Father

Our Father, who art in heaven,
hallowed be thy name;
thy kingdom come,
thy will be done
on earth as it is in heaven.
Give us this day our daily bread,
and forgive us our trespasses,
as we forgive those who trespass against us;
and lead us not into temptation,
but deliver us from evil.
Amen.

✒ Glory

Glory to the Father
and to the Son,
and to the Holy Spirit:
as it was in the beginning,
is now, and will be for ever. Amen.

Angel of God

Angel of God, my guardian dear,
to whom God's love entrusts me here;
ever this day, be at my side,
to light and guard, to rule and guide. Amen.

More Prayers . . .

Act of Contrition

My God,
I am sorry for my sins with all my heart.
In choosing to do wrong
and in failing to do good,
I have sinned against you
whom I should love above all things.
I firmly intend, with your help,
to do penance,
to sin no more,
and to avoid whatever leads me to sin.
Our Savior Jesus Christ
suffered and died for us.
In his name, my God, have mercy. Amen.

❧ Apostles' Creed

I believe in God,
the Father almighty,
Creator of heaven and earth,
and in Jesus Christ, his only Son, our Lord,
who was conceived by the Holy Spirit,
born of the Virgin Mary,
suffered under Pontius Pilate,
was crucified, died, and was buried;
he descended into hell;
on the third day he rose again from the dead;
he ascended into heaven,
and is seated at the right hand of God the Father almighty;
from there he will come to judge the living and the dead.
I believe in the Holy Spirit,
the holy catholic Church,
the communion of saints,
the forgiveness of sins,
the resurrection of the body,
and life everlasting. Amen.